IN
THE
EARLY
MORNING
RAIN

IN
THE
EARLY
MORNING
RAIN

Ted Berrigan

Cover & Drawings by
George Schneeman

Cape Goliard Press in association
with Grossman Publishers
New York

Grateful acknowledgement is hereby made to those editors interested enough in my work to have asked to print parts of it in their magazines & newspapers. I have tried to send poems to any editor interested enough to ask for them. Some of the poems herein have appeared in the following (mostly little) publications:

Angel Hair; The World; Cape Goliard Broadside Editions; The Iowa Defender; The White Dove Review; The Paris Review; "C" (A Journal of Poetry); Lines; Tom Clark's Once Series; Swing; Life Magazine; The New Yorker; The New York Herald Tribune; Adventures in Poetry; The Ant's Forefoot; The Park Review; Anonym; The Silver Cesspool; Entrails; Tzarad; Doones; The World Anthology; The Young American Poets Anthology; Suction; The Iowa Report; Telephone; Art & Literature; US; The University Review; Fuck You (A Magazine of the Arts); The Princeton Alumni Bulletin; Mother; Poets at Le Metro; Bean Spasms (Kulchur Press); Elephant; The Elephant's Ear; 2 Poets (Broadside with Anselm Hollo, printed by Tom Miller); Free Poems (Broadside printed by Nick Mikeloski); & Ten Short Poems for Anne Waldman, illustrated by George Schneeman). Fragment, from Cape Goliard Broadsides, was illustrated by Jim Dine. The five works subtitled Autobiography were published in Bill Berkson's Best & Co., illustrated by Joe Brainard. For any ommissions in this list, my apologies.

Ted Berrigan

This first edition was designed, printed and published by Cape Goliard Press, 10a Fairhazel Gardens, London N.W.6; of this edition 50 copies have been numbered and signed by the author.

Printed in Great Britain.

U.S. SBN paper 670 39685 0; cloth 670 39684 2
Library of Congress No. 77 127245

To my family
& friends

HELLO

"Hello"
originally
meant
"Be whole"
or
"Be healthy"

Today
it
simply
means
"Hello"

80TH CONGRESS

to Ron Padgett

It's 2 a.m. at Anne & Lewis's which is where it's at
On St. Mark's Place hash and Angel Hairs on our minds
Love is in our heart's (what else?) dope & Peter Schjeldahl
Who is new and valid in a blinding snowstorm

Inside joy fills our drugless shooting gallery
With repartee; where there's smoke there's marriage &, folks
That's also where it's at in poetry in 1967
Newly rich but still a hopeless invalid (in 1967)

Yes, it's 1967, & we've been killing time with life
But at Lewis & Anne's we live it "up"
Anne makes lovely snow-sodas while Lewis's watchamacallit warms up this
New Year's straight blue haze. We think about that

And money. With something inside us we float up
To & onto you, it, you were truly there & now you're here.

Ted Berrigan &
Dick Gallup

FRAGMENT

for Jim Brodey

Left behind in New York City, & oof!
That's the right one: sitting now, & I'm not thinking
Nor swishing; I'm just sitting. Getting over them two
Hamburgers. & that I think
Gets it all down. Here, anyway, I am
On this electric chair each breath nearer the last
Oceans of ripples solid under me: how come?
One pair of time-capsules trigger sweat
As one listens & one listening type types
LOOKS LIKE WE GONNA GET A LITTLE SNOW, HUH?
I don't know but you can bet something's going
    to happen.

THE CIRCLE

Up is waiting

Between is barely there

Down is alive

Now is spinning

It's a quick spin

Nevertheless

5 NEW SONNETS: A POEM

I

for Barry & Jacky Hall

His piercing pince-nez. Some dim frieze
dear Berrigan. He died
I, an island, sail, and my shores toss
to breathe an old woman slop oatmeal,
My babies parade waving their innocent flags
The taste of such delicate thoughts
Opulent, sinister, and cold!
Sing in idiom of disgrace
Dreams, aspirations of presence! Innocence gleaned,
annealed! The world in its mysteries are explained,
On the grass. To think of you alone
Your champion. Days are nursed on science fiction
For the fey Saint's parade   Today
Rivers of annoyance undermine the arrangements.

2

Hands point to a dim frieze, in the dark night.
Back to books. I read
on a fragrant evening, fraught with sadness
bristling hate.
And high upon the Brooklyn Bridge alone,
Huddled on the structured steps
The bulbs burn, phosphorescent, white,
Shall it be male or female in the tub?
Pale like an ancient scarf, she is unadorned,
and the struggles of babies congeal. A hard core is formed.
Suffering the poem of these states!
& you tremble at the books upon the earth
& he walks. Three ciphers and a faint fakir
No. One Two Three Four Today

3

It's 8:30 p.m. in New York and I've been running
Wind giving presence to fragments.
at every hand, my critic
Flinging currents into pouring streams
The bulbs burn phosphorescent, white
Fathers and teachers, and daemons down under the sea,
The singer sleeps in Cos.   Strange juxtaposed
"I wanted to be a cowboy." Doughboy will do
As my strength and I walk out and look for you
Winds flip down the dark path of breath
Released by night (which is not to imply   clarity
She is warm. Into the vast closed air of the slow
The wind's wish is the tree's demand
On the 15th day of November in the year of the motorcar.

4

Is there room in the room that you room in?
How much longer shall I be able to inhabit the Divine
deep in whose reeds great elephants decay;
loveliness that longs for butterfly! There is no pad
He buckles on his gun, the one
He wanted to know the *names*
And the green rug nestled against the furnace
Your hair moves slightly,
He is incomplete, bringing you Ginger Ale
The cooling wind keeps blowing, and
He finds he cannot fake
Wed to wakefulness, night which is not death
Fuscous with murderous dampness
But helpless, as blue roses are helpless.

& 5

Into the closed air of the slow
And then one morning to waken perfect-faced
The blue day!   In the air winds dance
Sleep half sleep half silence and with reason
banging around in a cigarette   she isn't "in love"
in my paintings for they are present
The withered leaves fly higher than dolls can see
A watchdog barks in the night
Francis Marion nudges himself gently into the big blue sky
What thwarts this fear I love
No lady dream around in any bad exposure
absence of passion, principles, love.   She murmurs
Is not genuine   it shines forth from the faces
littered with soup, cigarette butts, the heavy

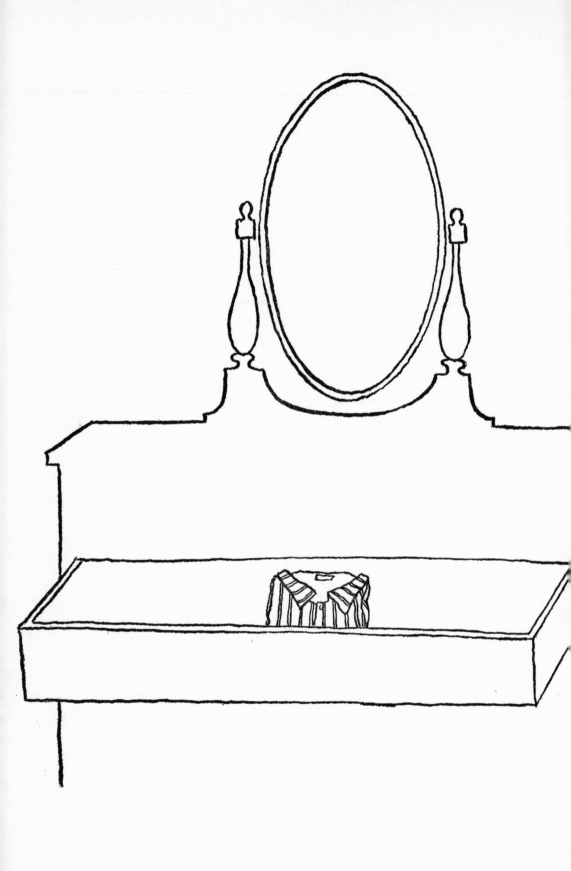

POEM

for Bill Berkson

Seven thousand feet over
The American Midwest
In the black and droning night
Sitting awake and alone
I worry the stewardess . . .
Would you like some coffee, sir?
How about a magazine?
No thanks. I smile and refuse.
My father died today. I
Fifteen hundred miles away
Left at once for home, having
received the news from mother
In tears on the telephone.
He never rode in a plane.

GUS

. . . Not far from here he was inside his head there were some sands. Of these
50 gave way to a room, latter resembling manure.

To the right, in a kit, a sort of woman-spanned pond absorbed water cake would
form at the bottom keep that in.

The hut rust bin thanks piece of colour.

A little pool gravel made him first step aside. Gus walked up under the arc-
light as far as the first person, perceived God. *She* was God, having lance, he
took her by the behind and kissed her butt. Gus want fuck, to get the information.
He spun off her dress. It was there, and
very beautiful,
his pecker.

Gus live entirely by hemselve and for hemselve.

He spen days taking off bottles, furnishing room, best system ea heat. For
Christ sake! Tryd smoke ham wash.

There was a large cop faggot pursued the secret butterfly near fourteen glass
jars tomato and green peas coated the stoppers with quicklime cheese wrapped
round with linen strip, then lunged into boiling water: it steamed. He por in
difference of temperature, he explode. Only, he were saved.

Then he poured some old sardine, laid veal cutlet inside, and sank the copper.
He ball him. He cold. He out again.

He continue the experiment. Shut up. The tin egg chicory lobster fish congratu-
late hemselve.

Ike Heraclitus, or, "Gus," still elusive, flit on ahead.

Despair defeat labor. The woman fell ill. She laid the copper. It glistens as if about to erupt. At that moment the secret fell in the eye, grace over the golden woman's form.

Then Gus made lunch.

PRESENCE

and I am lost in the ringing elevator
he waggles   the fat whiteness of milk
sweeping me to the top
one is remined of constellations
there there were pine needles
dreams of symbolism
the part that goes over the fence last
star light   the cord "reaches"
it was turkey
sheepish lights   you turned me on
reflecting dilemmas   majorities
Bildungsroman of the bathrobe ride
and the briny sound of the alarm
a funny feeling prompted me out of bed
Love
the top had been "sliced"
ribbons your presence on the white and green sheet
I asked for a Hook-and-Ladder
takes   The End.
in the ideal society pants

Now   we can make some explosions
shine like money
Francis is not diminutive   thanks
others are less legs
thighs wings breast
Caress the window grease, John
as you are not yet 12
19?   40?   who pulls me down?
that night we slept reverently   (you lust
I must lust in-
vigorating   the sixteen genre
dragon   bottle-opener
spiral cuff-link aerial
facade of the wonderful orient word
"doilies"

Overhead the moon is out
blacking my shoes, face

we were all livid, numinous

Things whip toward the center
licking the palate of his headache
this indicates your future
meditates on his wish which is
hooked onto the top and draped archly

Childhood fuses   a mystery play
Take off your beautiful blouse, you foolish girl!
which ribbons the marvelous laurel   the loop-
Are you list-   with this ring I
eye thee
(that was later, out west, after more baseball
some turkey
a wristwatch, dictionary, sniper suit, rifle
to "meditate"
(is there room in the tune to atune in?)

They were incensed at his arrival
Now we are glad   it was stinky
some paint them black in the face to be quaint or something
one symbol fact seems valid
I don't know
all hate it to be right
on the cards
which are sometimes funky (aesthetic) having
snow of feet and that a domination.
Then we had presence.

THE UPPER ARM

for Andy Warhol

Upon this field the physical energies of
Clouds.   He will no longer desire the
Demanding force, an incredible
Fortune has fallen across their paths.   I wait
a Prayer is paying for the art it releases
Prisoners from the hands
In an automobile accident on the
Face
And achieved enemy face
Paleface changed captive
Photographs later
Were tipped   "What does this mean, my son?"
Became categorical   as in "yes"   held on
The arms and
Powder on a little table
And down in a green forest ravine   near to "her"
Security of the relationship is made utterly
With high stakes and shot at those targets out of
Bows that spell
"MY PAINTINGS"

CORRIDORS OF BLOOD

1.   *Madrid*

a faint smile appears
shaking your beliefs
of which you have done no more
than sketch in the main outline
You are not a glutton for experience
There is a sudden buzz of activity
In the clear blue sky

2.   *Detective*

an enormous room with a balcony
less virulence
our labors were directed toward
    isolating and creating
such a pattern
"you must allow your feelings to
    float free, by
themselves, like dead leaves."
"I've got it."
we were furious

3.   Queen Matilda's Famous Tapestry

You got him out of your system
he was lying out of compassion
"Don't you see what it means?"
human society upside down
The second name
First we must retrieve our honor

4.   Henry VIII

women came down to breakfast
We saw that beautiful creature,
        Kay Francis, in
"Cynara"
the shabby taxis and peeling posters
teashops
and ugly window-dressing
a technical brilliance
I never saw the like of anywhere else

5.   Poe

"Merde" said Marco
in the apricot-coloured bar
Olga was in another bar
I am sure you understand
The captain lost his temper
A car drew up at the corner

6.   *Cattle of the Sun*

a profusion of melons, oranges and
        fish
all through that night
a lobster had been following him
I had an uncomfortable night
the only place I know
        where horror borders on poetry

7.   *The Death of Other*

should have "roots"
mass of ash-blonde hair
and black, clinging dresses
(the emotions: outline of
        a theory)
into her mouth
blistered strips of bladder
wrack

8.   *Czechoslovakia*

A red-tiled floor
thereafter we walked
sweeping, landscapes of white
limestone rock and
red rock
the most curious concoction
doubly oppressive
the sluggish heat:
I remember running

9.   *Hunger*

Irony and parody held pride of place
in her silk evening dress
Olga had several minor parts
little of Knut Hamsun
several bravura touches
"marking time"
treating it lightly
The death of Max Jacob

10.   *Henry IV*

naked
with a lion
a small lesbian
smoking a pipe
some silent young men
"Shit!" they exclaim
"Fuck all women!"
They all start singing patriotic songs

11.   *The Milk Bar*

Loud shouts and
running feet on the staircase
"Coward! Coward!"
the death of Robert Desnos
quite charming in a red and black dress
with black shoes
about three handbreadths high
The salesgirl laughs at us

12. Hate

I turned back
battered by the frightful air
But I made a kind of wager with myself
detail dazzled me
I considered making it
the theme of my next novel
Every day I had experience of this

13. American Films

a blue-eyed little girl with brown pigtails
their big red-tiled kitchen
big platefuls of bilberries for dessert
children's laughter
the fresh scent of wild berries
that little brown-haired girl
would be stood up against a wall
on richer, fiercer colors
    ocher, red, purple

14. Proust's Sex Life

it's "splendid animalism"
Ramon Fernandez made a special trip
to see
"Well," I said, "have you seen it?"
although I knew he was absolutely broke
my chosen themes had not lost
their sharpness

RUSTY NAILS

MY NAME

Smiling with grace the mother, the spouse, leaned
across to the fourth of their after-the-theatre party,
who was a girl older than this boy, aged almost seven ·
teen, by perhaps two years.

THE PROBLEM OF EVIL

I led in my childhood and youth the gently bred existence
of my class and my kind.

PATRIOTISM

An estimated two million wasps were loosed on an area
of four hundred and fifty miles inhabited by
eighty thousand people.

MY BEST FRIEND

That was about you in my story.

AN ORPHAN LEARNS TO COUNT

The Police swooped down in a squad car.

MALNUTRITION

By accident I met some rich homosexuals of the international queer set who cruise around the world, bumping into each other in queer joints from New York to Cairo.

CANCER

For there was a heavy curtain over the window, and in the center of the room, an electric light bulb, suspended from the ceiling, was all wrapped in newspaper.

SUNBURN

Loading his gun with one of these buttons, he seated himself on the bed beside his wife, and declared his intention of shooting the witch cat.

DEATH BY DROWNING

For, in respect to the latter branch of the supposition, it should be considered that the most trifling variation of the facts of the two cases might give rise to the most important miscalculations, by diverting thoroughly the two courses of events; very much as, in arithmetic, an error which, in its own individuality, may be inappreciable, produces, at length, by dint of multiplication at all points of the process, a result enormously at variance with the truth.

DEATH IN THE AFTERNOON

She sighed in vain for the chaff and the wheat, not knowing the one from the other.

MASSACRED BY THE INDIANS

Ain' nothin' new about that neither.

BAD NEWS

The man in bed — staring at me appraisingly — was enormous.

SPRING RETURNS

We are drawn to shit because we are imperfect in our uses of the good.

THE PENNILESS WIDOW

He drew his wife's attention to the pustule on the top of my skull for I had removed my hat out of courtesy.

THE DOORS OF PERCEPTION

There were seven to choose from, all putty.

THE TERRORS OF PUBERTY

She didn't realize her belly was more provocative when
it had been run through with hatred.

A PROVERB

Meanwhile the papers were reporting masochists shooting
tacks, with rubber bands, at apes in zoos.

A MESSAGE FROM THE LOVED ONE

I was horrified.

SYMBOLISM

He must have pressed the wrong button, or several of them,
for when the door fretted open he found himself deep under-
ground, with no heart to try again.

THE MODERN CRISIS

"What's this nasty piece of wood stuck in your boobs?"

THE AFTERLIFE

"The Cherry Orchard."

THE WORLD TODAY

"Jungle Law," the man agreed.

DEADLY VISIBLE RAYS

They had many days now when they were very happy.

SOMETHING'S HAPPENING HERE

Your historian will not attempt to list the sights he
pointed out in the multitudinous halls since no one will
ever forget them anyway.

EIGHT SQUARES

A good smell of hot coffee is coming out of the coffee-pot
on the table.

A GIFT

"You in the new winter
                    stretch forth your hands"

I AM A MAN OF CONSTANT SORROW

"I know from my own experience that telepathy is a fact."

Life of a Man

MATINEE

Morning
        (ripped out of my mind again!)

AS USUAL

Take off your hat & coat & give me all your money
I have to buy some pills & I'm flat broke

ON THE ROAD AGAIN

for Guisseppe Ungaretti

He called his Mama
Mohammed Scee-ab

He put his hand on
Her rear to be funny
She killed herself
You can bet no one ever told
His father

He made love to Frances
The talking mule

He's no sap either
He chopped her head off
So she can't yell and
He's plumb vanished

Let's go with him to Naples
To insult the old priest whose belly
Bulges over his belly-button
Like a piggy
And at number 5 Subnormal Street
We'll see his sad Victrola

You sap!
If you aren't turned on by now
It's your earache!

TONIGHT

Winds in the stratosphere
Apologise to the malcontents
Downstairs

JOY OF SHIPWRECKS

The torpedo was friendly
it buggered us

Mayday!

The climax came later
In the water
Near a sea-horse

AFTER BREAKFAST

Flame & Fury
The colt and the dolt became outlaws

The automobile slew them

DECEMBER

Brother and sister departed
With apologies to the mother for intercourse
In their hearts

A REPLY TO THE FRAGILE

If he bites you he's friendly
If it hurts you
Go away
Don't give him a fresh try
Unless you have titties
Like a fast horse

TOBACCO

He made coffee
In his maid's uniform

He made coffee with animals
From the desert
Who expectorated into the coffeepot

His veins swelled up with an army
Of germs whose unconscious's
Hated these possibilities

He reared back saying, "Me Nasty!"
So We began to BE Nasty

As for what happened next
You can bet that he learned to express himself

TOOTING MY HORN ON DUTY

Tooting my horn on duty in the infantry
Made my name mud   PU
In the army I had nosebleeds

The Infantry was so distracting
It kindled up in my nose
An invisible odor
That hindered my toots

One day while on duty
I rammed into a chestnut
And got blood all over my flute
Not to mention this nosebleed

I spat out so many teeth I knew it was an omen
The vitamins I had to take made me ill
Ten blood transfusions   It was almost all over
When two big rocks stopped the bleeding

This was my unhappy childhood

CORPORAL PELLEGRINI

He was ugly

She kissed the poor fellow
On his belly

ai-yai-yai

Wild horses couldn't hold him

He snaked her carcass
Around a finger
Like a bowling ball

Come and get it!

They threw him in the pen
And busted his illusions
On the fires of Corregidor

His rifle slowly
Fired
Better and better

Killing the idiot

LIFE AMONG THE WOODS

Near Paris, there is a boat. Near this boat live the beautiful Woods.

They are a charming family, the Woods, very friendly: Mr. Woods, Mrs. Woods, their son Peter, and their tiny daughter, Bubbles.

Mr. Woods is very rich. He has a grand house, in four pieces: a kitchen, a stable, a room for lying down, and a room for infants. In this house there is, in addition, a brain room.

Mr. Woods' garden is also very grand. It is full of lettuces, flowers and fruits.

Mrs. Woods likes cooking plenty. She makes pies, pots of tea, and desserts. The little Woods have beautiful appetites. They eat a lot.

Mrs. Woods' kitchen is very appropriate. It has a pretty little furnace, a table, four chaise lounges and a large placard. On the placard there are six S's, six tassels, and fifty soupspoons. (One of the soupspoons is crusty.) There is also a grand casserole.

In the room for laying down there are four tiny books, four chaise lounges and four tiny tables. One sometimes goes to the toilet on the tables.

In the room for infants there is a big table, plenty of chaise lounges and one grand placard on which are pictures of the toys of the tiny Woods: a puppy, a train, a toupee', a cigarette, some balls, some books, a pellet, soap, a strangler's cord, and lots of other things.

The black bag and the wise man may be found in the brain room.

They eat in the stable, where there is a grand table and some chaise lounges.

Mrs. Woods' rat poison is kept in the stable, in a great bottle.

In her office she keeps plenty of other things. She keeps bread, berries, beer, lace, celery, buttons, plums, and a comforter.

IN THREE PARTS

for John Giorno

According
to
the
basic
law
of
visual
perception
any
stimulus
pattern
tends
to
be
seen
in
such
a
way
that
the
resulting
pattern
is
as
simple
as
the
given
conditions
permit.

Before
the
orgasmic
platform
in
the
outer
third
of
the
vagina
develops
sufficiently
to
provide
increased
exteroceptive
and
proprioceptive
stimulation
for
both
sexes,
the
over-
distended
excitement-
phase
vagina
gives
many
women
the
sensation
that
the
fully
erect
penis
is
"lost
in
the
vagina."

With
daring
and
strength
men
like
Pollock,
deKooning
Tobey,
Rothko,
Smith
and
Kline
filled
their
work
with
the
drama,
anger,
pain,
and
confusion
of
contemporary
life.

IN 4 PARTS

A person can lie around on an uncrowded beach

And when too much peace and quiet gets on his
nerves, he can always get dressed and tour Israel.

*

Mayor
Frank
X.
Graves
today
ordered
the
arrest
of
Allen
Ginsberg
if
the
police
could
prove
that
the
poet
smoked
marijuana
while
looking
at
the
Passaic
Falls
yesterday.

The
Jewish
Memorial
Hospital's
Junior
League
will
give
its
second
annual
discotheque
benefit
Sunday
at
the
Round
Table.

*

William
Carlos
Williams
the
Paterson
N. J.
physician
was
a
strong
and
vigorous
poet
who
spoke
in
the
American
idiom.

AN AUTOBIOGRAPHY IN 5 PARTS

CRAZE MAN WILIIKER

for Pierre Reiter

Once there was a rich man named craze man Wiliiker. This man was
always very nice he would give alot of money to poor people,
but he said to himselve "I had better save some of my money for my-
selve." So the next day he went to the bank with a gun (just in case
they would not give him his money) he said "give me my money be-
cause I have to buy presents for all my relatives."

The next day he went to the Monkey Wards department store he
bought a 24 foot yate, a motercycle, a small car, a byicycle, and meny
more expencive gifts. Then he went to the store and bought a big air-
plane for himself then he loaded up his airplane and flew through the
city tos money all over.

The next day he had a pipeline put on the hot plains so people in
distress could get water all through that area. He also built little shops
into skyscrapers for the LandLord. He built hospitals all over the earth.

One day while flying around in his airplane he ran accross two men
trying to sell old pots, but they were not having any bissness. He land-
ed and he asked them "Hows bissness?" The men replied "We've been
here more than 40 days and haven't sold a pot." Wiliikers sayed "I'll
buy your whole stock and as meny more pots as you can get." The
man gave him his bill and supplyed him with his pots.

Two days later he took his wife out to dinner and tiped the waiter a
hundred dollarbill. He invited all the hobbos he knew to dinner and
he even told the manager that he was going to give the biggest party the
world has ever known and that it would be held on December 25. He
sayed it would be adverticed all over the earth. When December 25
came all the men asked him why he was so nice to everybody he said
"It's because it's Christmas day. *Merry Christmas!*

from MEMOIRS

Never will I forget that trip. The dead were so thick in spots we tumbled over them. There must have been at least 2000 of those sprawled bodies. I identified the insignia of six German divisions, some of their best. The stench was carnal to the point of suffocation. The sounds and cries of wounded men sounded everywhere. I could but think how wrong I'd been one bright day at Texas Military Academy when I had so glibly criticized Dante's description of hell as too extreme.

A flare suddenly lit up the scene for a fraction of a minute and we hit the dirt hard. There just ahead of us stood three Germans—a lieutenant pointing with outstretched arm, a sergeant crouched over a machine gun, a corporal feeding a bandolier of cartridges to the weapon. I held my breath waiting for the burst. But there was nothing. My guide shifted his poised grenade to the other hand and reached for his flashlight.

The Germans had not moved. They were never to move. They were dead, all dead—the lieutenant with shrapnel through his heart, the sergeant with his belly blown into his back, the corporal with his spine where his head should have been. We left them there, gallant men dead in the service of their country.

I completed my reconnaissance and reached our flank regiment just before dawn. There I found its distinguished colonel, Frank McCoy, and its gallant chaplain, Father Duffy, just returned from burying the poet Sergeant Joyce Kilmer beside the stump of one of those trees he had immortalized.

A LETTER

to John Giorno

When Wyn & Sally and the twins went to Minnesota to visit Wyn's father last August, Wyn discovered marijuana growing wild all over the Minnesota country-side. He brought back a suitcase full and said to me, "How would you like to go out and harvest some?" So in the middle of September, when the moon was right just before the first frost, we flew out to Minneapolis at 10:30 in the morning with five large suitcases and a trunk. I was dressed in an old Brooks Brothers suit and a vest. We arrived in Minneapolis at 2, were met by a white Hertz rent-a-car and drove 2 hours to Red Wing. All along the side of the road and in front of every farmhouse were these 12 foot high clusters. Wyn said they're so dumb out there they think that marijuana comes from Mexico. We cased this sand pit and it looked OK. Then we emptied the 5 suitcases and the trunk which were filled with the costumes from "Conquest of the Universe" into a garbage dump and drove to Frontenac where Mark Twain spent his summers. We bought 2 bathing suits and went for a swim in the Mississippi. It was terrific. Then we drove to Lake City which is this 1930's Bonnie & Clyde town and we sat in this 1930's soda-fountain cafe waiting for it to get dark. We telephoned Sally and told her everything was going great. Then we drove back to the sand pit and parked the car behind a falling down shed of an abandoned turkey farm and sat watching how many cars passed on the road. When it got dark, we changed into dungarees and went to work. I cut the plants and Wyn cut them into small pieces and stuffed them into plastic bags. There was this jungle of pot plants that looked like giant Christmas Trees and moonlight and dew, and the dew and resin got all over my skin and I was stoned. About 3 AM we changed back into the straight clothes and drove to Minneapolis. We didn't take any amphetamine because I thought we'd look suspicious if we looked like speed freaks at 6 in the morning. I was so tired I just went up to the ticket counter and said to the guy, "Here!" We flew back to NY with 70 pounds of wet grass. It dried down to 24 pounds.

CHE GUEVARA'S CIGARS

Guevara had noticed me smoking, and had remarked that of course I would never dare smoke Cuban cigars. I told him that I would love to smoke Cuban cigars but that Americans couldn't get them. The next day, a large polished-mahogany box hand-inlaid with the Cuban seal and amid swirling patterns in the national colors, flying a tiny Cuban flag from a brass key, and crammed with the finest Havanas arrived at my room. With it was a typewritten note from Guevara, reading in Spanish, "Since I have no greeting card, I have to write. Since to write to an enemy is difficult, I limit myself to extending my hand." (I took the box, the cigars untouched, back to Washington and showed it to President Kennedy. He opened it and asked, "Are they good?" "They're the best," I said, whereupon he took one out of the box, lit it, and took a few puffs. Then he looked up at me suddenly and said, "You should have smoked the first one.")

FRANK O'HARA'S QUESTION
FROM "WRITERS AND ISSUES"
JOHN ASHBERY

what sky
out there is between the ailanthuses
a 17th century prison an aardvark
a photograph of Mussolini and
a personal letter from Isaak Dinesen
written after eating

can be succeeded by a calm evaluation
of the "intense inane" that surrounds
him:

it is cool
I am high
and happy
as it turns
on the earth
tangles me
in the air

and between these two passages (from
the long poem "Biotherm") occurs a me-
diating line which might stand to charac-
terize all of Mr. O'Hara's art:

I am guarding it from mess and message.

Ted Berrigan

ENTRANCE

for Ed Dorn

               10 years of boot
               Take it away
               & it's off
               Under the table
                  2
                & I'm hovering
               I'm above *American Language*
                               one foot
               is expressing itself as continuum
               the other, sock

groan   I am dog
       tired from cake
walking
       to here.   That is,
       An Entrance.

MARCH 17TH, 1970

Someone who loves me calls me
      & I just sit, listening

Someone who likes me wires me,
      to do something. I'll do it

Tomorrow.

Someone who wants to do me harm
      is after me
& finds me.

I need to kill someone.
      And that's what it's all about.
         Right Now.

"IN THREE PARTS"

blank mind part

Sounds pretty sane to me!

never thought of that!

Part two

Excursions across the ice

Confusions of the cloth

bread & butter
bread & butter

kiss kiss

Part Three

LOVE

Addenda: Sleep

Oh, hello, Ted!

EPITHALAMION

Pussy put her paw into the pail of paint.
"Hip, hop, pip, pop, tip, top, pop-corn".
The dipper tipped and the sirup dripped upon her apron.
Phillippa put the Parson's parcel beside the Professor's papers.
Bowser buried his bone inside a barrel.
The brown bear stole the bumblebee.
White snow whirled everywhere.
The able laborer objects to the bride.
Adam and Eve stumbled over the rubber tube.
Mama made a muffler and a muff for me.
My Mary's asleep by the murmuring stream
The meadow-mouse uses the lamp for its moonbeam.

In Minneapolis, Minnesota there are many married men.
Many Americans are making money in Mexico.

HOMECOMING

I sit on   fat
                                      like
An old dog
Anxious to set.   Across
          the fields   fruit
grows   in
Another state. The map
Goes quietly dark. In the
      corners   white
          jasmine blossoms begin
To radiate
Cold.   In the sky the
Soft, loose
          stars swarm.
                              Now
                drops of blood squirt
Onto the stiff leaves.
          Now I
breathe.

POOP

Nature makes my teeth "to hurt"
*
Each conviction lengthens the sentence
*
Women are interesting when I look at them
*
Art is medicine for imbeciles
*
Great Art is a Great Mistake
*
If it's inspiration you want, drop your panties
*
If I fall in love with my friend's wife, she's fucked*

                        *alternates:

                                    I'm fucked
                                    he's fucked

AMERICAN EXPRESS

Cold rosy dawn in New York City
                                        not for me
in Ron's furlined Jim Bridger
                                        (coat)
that I borrowed two years ago
                                        had cleaned
but never returned, Thank god!
                                        On 6th Street
Lunch poems burn
                        a hole is in my pocket
two donuts one paper bag
                        in hand
hair is in my face and in my head is
                                        "cold rosy dawn in New York City"

I woke up this morning
                        it was night
you were on my mind
                        on the radio
And also there was a letter
                        and it's to you
if "you" is Ron Padgett,
                        American express
shivering now in Paris
                        Oklahoma
two years before
                        buying a new coat for the long trip
back to New York City
                        that I'm wearing now

It is cold in here
                        for two
looking for the boll weevil

                    (looking for a home), one with pimples
one blonde, from Berkeley
                    who says, "Help!" and
"Hey, does Bobby Dylan come around here?"
                                        "No, man," I say,
"Too cold!"
            & they walk off, trembling,
                                (as I do in L. A.)
so many tough guys, faggots, & dope addicts!
                                though I assure them
"Nothing like that in New York City!"
                            It's all in California!
(the state state)
            that shouldn't be confused with
                            The balloon state
that I'm in now
            hovering over the radio
                            following the breakfast of champions
& picking my curious way
                    from left to right
                            across my own white
            expansiveness

            MANHATTAN!

        listen

    The mist of May
                is on the gloaming
& all the clouds
            are halted, still
                        fleecey
            & filled
                    with holes.

    They are alight with borrowed warmth,

                                just like me.

FEBRUARY AIR

for Donna Dennis

Can't cut it (night)
                    in New York City
            it's alive
inside my tooth
                on St. Mark's Place
        where exposed nerve
                        jangles

                *

that light
isn't on
            for me
                    that's it
                            though you are
                            right here.

                *

        It's RED RIVER
        time
                on tv

and
Andy's BRILLO BOX is on
the icebox is on   High
                too   over St. Nazaire, the
                                            Commando is poised

                                            that means tonight's raid
                                                        is "on"
                The Monkee
                at the typewriter
                is turned on

        (but the tooth hurts)
                            You'd Better Move On

BLACK POWER

It's ritzy   Thrift,

Horn & Hardart's is
too, one
cup of coffee, black
                away from it

& Generosity
though commingling with incontrovertible hard- (art)
headedness
            does warm

& it keeps it up

            e.g.

                "Art is art & life is
                Life." Fairfield Porter said
            that:

                    & That means

                    Coffee

                    Black as on
            57th Street

            The Hotel Buckingham (facade) is

looming over lunch   poems   & I
looming over coffeecup   white   two eyes
looming over Joe's black & yellow polka-dots

            (a tie)

    that once belonged to Montgomery Clift:

It's all mine now, is saved, knowing
That, & that happily being that

                        "the living is easy"
            Tho the art is hard,
    sometimes, to see
                    through so much looming.

        More coffee may save me that.

THE TEN GREATEST BOOKS OF THE YEAR, 1968

The Collected Earlier Poems by William Carlos Williams
Selected Writings Charles Olson
Chicago Review One Dollar
Alkahest
New American Writing No. 1
THE RANDOM HOUSE DICTIONARY OF THE ENGLISH LANGUAGE
The Pocket Aristotle
After Dinner We take A Drive Into The Night by Tony Towle
Love Poems (Tentative Title) by Frank O'Hara
The Sky Pilot in No Man's Land by Ralph Connors
Cosmic Consciousness by Dr. Richard Bucke
Meditations On The Signs of The Zodiac by John Jocelyn

In Public In Private by Edwin Denby

The World Number 1   Cover by Dan Clark
The World Number 2   Cover by Robert McMillan
The World Number 3   Cover by George Schneeman
The World Number 4   Cover by Donna Dennis
The World Number 5   Cover by Jack Boyce
The World Number 6   Cover by Fielding Dawson
The World Number 7   Cover by Bill Beckman
The World Number 8   Cover by George Schneeman
The World Number 9   Cover by Joe Brainard
The World Number 10   Cover by Larry Fagin
The World Number 11   Cover by Tom Clark
The World Number 12   Cover by George Schneeman
The World Number 13   Cover by Donna Dennis
The World Number 14   Cover by Joe Brainard

WATERLOO SUNSET

We ate lunch, remember? and I paid the check
Under trees in rain of false emotion and big bull
With folks going in and out putting words in our mouths that are
shouting, "Hurrah for Bristol Cream!" We threw a leave-sandwich
Into the sunlight—it greedily gobbled it up, and growing brighter
Emanating from their glasses came the little drinkies
Reflections of the magazine Grandma edits
On whose pages a bouquet is blossoming sort of. You bounced a check
Into years of lives down under the weather vane, barf!
The influence of alcohol rebounded 500 miles into Africa.

But a little drinkie never hurt nobody, except an African.
The Earth sops up liquids, I mean drinks,
And is tipsy as pinballs on the ocean
Wobbling on its axis. We turn a paleface shade of white
In the rain that pelts the doo-doo
That flies from the eyes' blinds. It doesn't matter though
                on the sweet side
Of the moon. Don't be a horrible sourpuss
Moon! Have a drink
Have an entire issue! Waves goodbye & reels, into sun
Of light dark light roll over Beethoven
Our shelter-half misses your shelter-half. There's nothing left
                of love
But we have checkerberry leaves
Mint, Juniper, tree-light
Elder-flowers, sweet goldenrod, bugspray & Juice.

And you are a pretty girl-boy
And I am a pretty man-woman
and we are here-there
In England and the food is absolutely cold-hot.
In the aromatic sundown, according to the magazine version
Or automatic sundown   English words are a gas
Slurring the Earth's one heaving angel turns in unison
& paddles your rear gently as befits one in love
            with you & I
No change   My face is all right

For us. We are bored through & we are through with you
With our professionalism (you have to become useless to drink).

All we ever wanted to do in the rosy sunlight was
In the first place was . . . was . . . was . . . uh
Run our fingers through your curly hair
Ooops! No, not that. I mean all
We really wanted to do was jazz yr mother
Fight off insects & sing a sad solitary tune
On the excellencies of Bristol Cream
Six dollars a bottle Praise The Lord

Ted Berrigan & Ron Padgett

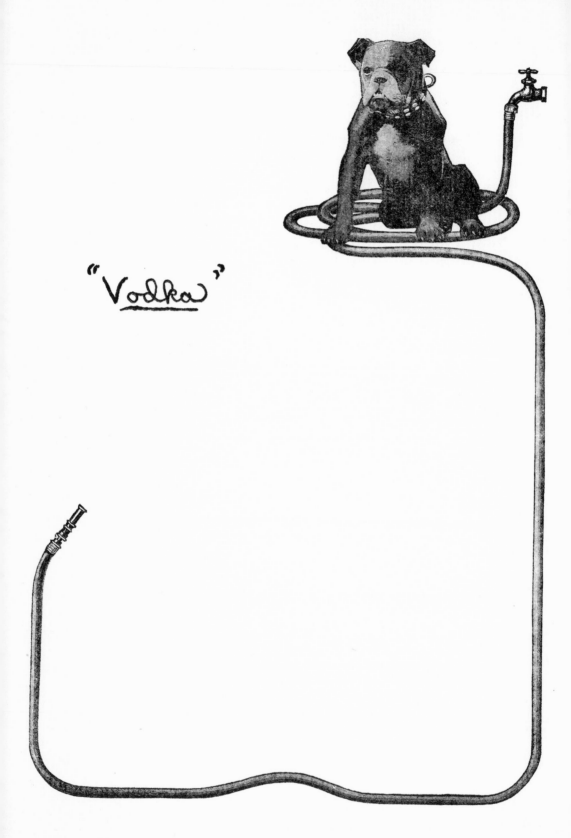

"Vodka"

30

The fucking enemy shows up

interstices

bent

GREY MORNING

Rain
Coming down
Outside her
Windows
I can be seen inside
                    the drops
                    of rain
                    falling
                    limping
                    This girl in mind.

THINGS TO DO IN ANNE'S ROOM

Walk right in

        sit right down

                baby, let your hair hang down

        It's on my face that hair
        & I'm amazed to be here
        the sky outside is green the blue
        shows thru the trees

        I'm on my knees

                unlace Li'l Abner
            shoes
                place them under the bed
                    light cigarette
            study out the dusty bookshelves,

                        sweat

Now I'm going to do it

        SELF RELIANCE
        THE ARMED CRITIC
        MOBY DICK
        THE WORLD OF SEX
        THE PLANET OF THE APES

Now I'm going to do it

        deliberately

           take off clothes
        shirt goes on the chair
        pants go on the shirt
        socks next to shoes next to bed

the chair goes next to the bed

get into the bed
  be alone
suffocate
don't die

    & it's that easy.

THE GREAT GENIUS

The Great Genius is
A man who can do the
Average thing when everybody
Else is going crazy.

POEM FOR PHILIP WHALEN

(About Emily Dickinson)

What about Emily Dickinson?

DEAD FINGERS TALK

I've got a lot of things to do today.

For example write this poem.
She's Terrific.

Now, this poem is to say that

                                       period?
              ***   colon?
                                  space??

Lord I wonder just exactly what can happen oh Hello, Pill . . .

It's a terrific spelling problem there's two kinds of L's (on the typewriter)
and *that* is a good example of the way some people
think

(NOVEL)

This here, now is what I'm trying to say it's a sonnet. A kind of formal BEAN
SPAS
She goes all over the place, eh?   M.
ROOT   RAINBOW HA-HA
She's so fine:

You Didn't Even Try

HEROIN

(2) photographs of Anne

             80 years old

                       lovely, as always

                               a child

                 under an old fashion

                              duress

A Bibliography of Works
by Jack Kerouac

                A white suit
                  and a black dress
                    w/ high-necked
                        mini-skirt

        strolling

      two by two

across   a   brown   paper   bag

          above   The Relation Ship

Warm white thighs   & floating bend   gia pronto

     my heart is filled with light

          this

Life
that is
one, tho
the Lamps
be many   & proud   & there's a breeze sort of
          lightly moving the top

     of yr head

&   I'm going
                                        way over
                                      the white
                                                skyline

                               & I'll do
                           what I want to

                     & you can't keep me here

          & the streets are theirs now

                        & the tempo's

                               &   the space

ANTI-WAR POEM

It's New Year's Eve, of 1968, & a time
for Resolution.

I don't like Engelbert Humperdink.

I love the incredible String Band.

The War goes on
                   & war is Shit.

I'll sing you a December song.

It's 5 below zero in Iowa City tonight.

This year I found a warm room
That I could go to
                be alone in
& never have to fight.

I didn't live in it.

I thought a lot about dying
But I said *Fuck it*.

TOUGH BROWN COAT

to Jim Carroll

Tough brown coat
Tie with red roses
Green cord vest

Brown stripes
on soft white
shirt

white T-shirt

White man,
   Tomorrow you die!

"You kidding me?"

BABE RAINBOW

Light up

smoke

burn a few holes in the blanket

Burn a few holes in the Yellow blanket

burning

smoking

reading

IT'S IMPORTANT

It's important not
to back out
of the mirror:

You will be great, but
You will be queer.

It's a complication.

DIAL-A-POEM

Inside
The homosexual sleeps
long past day break
We won't see him
awake
                this time around.

IN MY ROOM

Green   (grass)

    A white house   brown
                                 mailbox

        (Friendly pictures)

                *

TELEVISION   snow

                           (that's outside)

   No-mind

                     No messages

     (Inside)

Thanksgiving   1969

ANN ARBOR ELEGY

for Franny Winston d. sept 27th, 1969

Last night's congenial velvet sky
Conspired that Merrill, Jayne, Deke, you & I
Get it together at Mr. Flood's Party, where we got high
On gin, shots of scotch, tequila salt & beer
Talk a little, laugh a lot, & turn a friendly eye
On anything that's going down beneath Ann Arbor's sky
Now the night's been let to slip its way
Back toward a mild morning's gray
A cool and gentle rain is falling, cleaning along my way
To where Rice Krispies, English muffins, & coffee, black
Will make last night today. We count on that, each new day
Being a new day, as we read what the Ann Arbor News
        has to say.

SONG: PROSE & POETRY

to Alice Notley

My heart is confirmed in it's pure Buddhahood
But a heavy list to starboard
$$\text{makes me forget}$$
From time to time.
$$\text{Breath makes a half turn}$$
Downward & divides:
$$\text{it doesn't add up}$$
2 plus 2 equals 1:   It's fun, yes,
But it isn't true, &
I can't love you
$$\text{this way.}$$

2.

So, what'll I do, when you
$$\text{are far away}$$
& I'm so blue?
$$\text{I'll wait.}$$
$$\text{& I'll be true some day.}$$

3.

That's all well & good. But
What happens in the mean time?

WAKE UP

Jim Dine's toothbrush eases two pills
activity under the clear blue sky; girl
for someone else in white walk by
it means sober up, kick the brunette out of bed
going out to earn your pay; it means out;
bells, ring; squirrel, serve a nut; daylight
fade; fly resting on your shoulder blades
for hours; you've been sleeping, taking it easy
neon doesn't like that; having come your way
giving you a free buzz, not to take your breath away
just tightening everything up a little; legs
pump; head, wobble; tongue, loll; fingers, jump;
drink; eat; flirt; sing; speak;
night time ruffles the down along your cheek

ERASABLE PICABIA

The front is hiding the rear
*
The heart of a man
is not as great as an amphitheater
*
Spinoza is the one who threw a pass to Lou Spinoza
*
There is no death
there is only dissolution
*
love of hate
is totally great
*
me, I disguise myself as a man
in order to laugh
*
I have always loved
a serious jackoff scene
*
infantile paralysis is the beginning of wisdom
*
everything is poison
except our meat
*
Flowers and candy make my teeth ache
*
The most beautiful and most noble
of men are queers
*
get the pussy
*
mystical expalations are dopey

Aunt Winnie fingers the thunder to learn,
so that we have left everything aside
but not as a cloud mind steps beside
    the slow reservoir
now it is all of this, the pink bulbs included,
which means we have "protected ourselves"
by forgetting all we were dealt

by **Ted Berringan**
& **Jim Carrol**

IN BED

I love all the girls

    I've been in bed with

I even love those

    who preferred not to do anything

once there:

Tho it seems to me now

    they were nuts!

(the latter)

    in bed.

EASY LIVING

to David Henderson

I hope to go
              everywhere
       in good time:
                  Going's a pleasure,
           being someplace
                       & then
           Many Happy Returns

                    *

But Africa,
          I don't know
     all that heat
                all the time
even when it's raining
                 all the time . . .

                    *

I've always found heat
                    constant heat
                             difficult
       to get inside of
                  & not to mention
          impossible to avoid . . .

                    *

You don't have to do anything you don't want to.
              That's true.

                    *

     Go now   /   Pay later

                    *

Equally—You can do anything you want to.
                     Yes, I know that.

*

But Africa:

      well, I do know one thing
   for sure:

      It would be tremendous
  Africa

    going there
  to go there with

        David Henderson!
(Just like Pittsburgh).

LIKE POEM

to Joan Fagin

Joan,
I like you
         plenty.

You'd do
         to ride the river with.

I take these tiny pills
to our love.

         Plenty.

Then I drink up the river.
Be seeing you.

PEACE

What to do
        when the days' heavy heart
                having risen, late
in the already darkening East
            & prepared at any moment, to sink
                      into the West
surprises suddenly,
        & settles, for a time,
              at a lovely place
where mellow light spreads
          evenly
            from face to face?

The days' usual aggressive
          contrary beat
              now softly dropped
into a regular pace
        the head riding gently its personal place
where pistons feel like legs
          on feelings met like lace.
                Why,
take a walk, then,
        across this town. It's a pleasure
to meet one certain person you've been counting on
              to take your measure
who will smile, & love you, sweetly, at your leisure.
              And if
she turns your head around
        like any other man,
            go home
and make yourself a sandwich
        of toasted bread, & ham
              with butter
lots of it
    & have a diet cola,
        & sit down
& write this,
      because you can.

HALL OF MIRRORS

to Kristin Lems

We miss something now
as we think about it
Let's see: eat, sleep & dream, read
A good book, by Robert Stone
Be alone

Knew of it first
in New York City. Couldn't find it
in Ann Arbor, though
I like it here
Had to go back to New York
Found it on the Upper West Side
there

I can't live with you
But you live
here in my heart
You keep me alive and alert
aware of something missing
going on

I woke up today just in time
to introduce a poet
then to hear him read his rhymes
so unlike mine   & not bad
as I'd thought another time

no breakfast, so no feeling fine.

Then I couldn't find the party, afterwards
then I did
then I talked with you.

Now it's back

& a good thing for us
It's letting us be wise, that's why
it's being left up in the air

You can see it, there
as you look, in your eyes

Now it's yours & now it's yours & mine.
We'll have another look, another time.

ANN ARBOR SONG

I won't be at this boring poetry reading
    again!
I'll never have to hear
    so many boring poems again!
& I'm sure I'll never read them again:
In fact, I haven't read them yet!

Anne won't call me here again,
To tell me that Jack is dead.
I'm glad you did, Anne, though
It made me be rude to friends.
I won't cry for Jack here again.

& Larry & Joan won't visit me here
    again.
Joan won't cook us beautiful dinners,
    orange & green & yellow & brown
    here again.
& Thom Gunn & Carol & Don & I won't get high
    with Larry & Joan here again
Though we may do so somewhere else again.

Harris & John & Merrill won't read
    in my class, again.
Maybe there'll never be such a class
    again:
I think there probably will, though
& I know Allen will follow me round the world
    with his terrible singing voice:
But it will never make us laugh here again.

You Can t Go Home Again is a terrific book:
I doubt if I'll ever read that again.
(I read it first in Tulsa, in 1958)
& I'll *never* go there again.

Where does one go from here? Because
I'll go somewhere again. I'll come somewhere again, too,
& You'll be there, & together we can have a good time.
Meanwhile, you'll find me right here, when you
                    come through, again.

PEOPLE WHO DIED

Pat Dugan........my grandfather........throat cancer........1947.

Ed Berrigan........my dad........heart attack........1958.

Dickie Budlong........my best friend Brucie's big brother, when we were
                             five to eight........killed in Korea, 1953.

Red O'Sullivan........hockey star & cross-country runner
                    who sat at my lunch table
                          in High School......car crash......1954.

Jimmy "Wah" Tiernan........my friend, in High School,
                    Football & Hockey All-State......car crash....1959.

Cisco Houston........died of cancer........1961.

Freddy Herko, dancer....jumped out of a Greenwhich Village window in 1963.

Anne Kepler....my girl....killed by smoke-poisoning while playing
                  the flute at the Yonkers Children's Hospital
                  during a fire set by a 16 year old arsonist....1965.

Frank......Frank O'Hara......hit by a car on Fire Island, 1966.

Woody Guthrie......dead of Huntington's Chorea in 1968.

Neal......Neal Cassady......died of exposure, sleeping all night
                       in the rain by the RR tracks of Mexico....1969.

Franny Winston........just a girl....totalled her car on the Detroit-Ann Arbor
                  Freeway, returning from the dentist....Sept. 1969.

Jack......Jack Kerouac......died of drink & angry sicknesses....in 1969.

My friends whose deaths have slowed my heart stay with me now.

TELEGRAM

to Jack Kerouac

Bye-Bye Jack.

See you soon.